LOOKING AFTER YOUR PET

Guinea Pig

Text by Clare Hibbert

Photography by Robert and Justine Pickett

A+

Titles in the LOOKING AFTER YOUR PET series:

• Cat • Dog • Hamster • Rabbit
• Guinea Pig • Fish

First published in 2003 by Hodder Wayland
338 Euston Road, London NW1 3BH
Hodder Wayland is an imprint of Hodder
Children's Books.
This edition published under license from
Hodder Wayland. All rights reserved.

Produced by White-Thomson Publishing Ltd.
2/3 St. Andrew's Place, Lewes, BN7 1UP
Copyright © 2004 White-Thomson Publishing

Editor: Elaine Fuoco-Lang, Interior Design:
Leishman Design, Cover design: Hodder Wayland,
Photographs: Robert Pickett, Proofreader: Alison
Cooper

Published in the United States by
Smart Apple Media
1980 Lookout Drive, North Mankato,
Minnesota 56003

Library of Congress Cataloging-in-Publication
Data

Hibbert, Clare, 1970–
Guinea pig / text by Clare Hibbert ; photography
by Robert and Justine Pickett.
p. cm. — (Looking after your pet)
Summary: Introduces pet care for guinea pigs,
including such topics as feeding, grooming, and
visit to the veterinarian.
ISBN 1-58340-434-1
1. Guinea pigs as pets—Juvenile literature. 2.
Guinea pigs as pets—Health—Juvenile literature.
[1. Guinea pigs. 2. Pets.] I. Pickett, Robert, ill. II.
Pickett, Justine, ill. III. Title.

SF459.G9H53 2004
636.935'92—dc22   2003062394

9 8 7 6 5 4 3 2 1

Acknowledgments
The publishers would like to thank the following
for their assistance with this book:
The PDSA (Reg. Charity 283483) for their help
and assistance with the series.

With kind thanks for guinea pigs to
Rosie Pilbrim and The Animal Care Unit,
Canterbury College.

The Web site addresses (URLs) included in this
book were valid at the time the book went to
press. However, because of the nature of the
Internet, it is possible that some addresses may
have changed, or sites may have changed or
closed down since publication.

Printed in China

Contents

Keeping guinea pigs

The first question to ask yourself is, "Why do I want guinea pigs?"

Guinea pigs can be shy at first, but they make great pets. When they get to know you, they love being cuddled. But before you decide guinea pigs are the pets for you, be sure you will be able to look after them. You will have to buy a comfortable hutch and a run so they can play in the yard.

▶ You will need to handle your pet guinea pig every day.

4

Top Tips

🐾 Do you want guinea pigs with short, rough, or long hair? They all make wonderful pets!

🐾 You should keep more than one guinea pig; one may get lonely.

🐾 Never keep males and females together. You will end up with lots of baby guinea pigs.

...uinea pigs with rough or long hair need daily ...ooming. This is a rough-haired guinea pig.

...nea pigs usually live four or five years, ... can live to be as old as eight. You will ...d to feed and handle your pets every ... for all those years. You will also need ... lean out their hutch and find ...eone to look after them when ... go on vacation.

...wo guinea pigs are better ...an one. They will keep each ...her company.

5

Choosing your pet

Buy healthy baby guinea pigs.

First, decide where to get your guinea pigs. Try a pet shop, breeder, or animal shelter. Or maybe you know someone who has baby guinea pigs, called puppies, in need of a good home. It is best to get young guinea pigs that are five to six weeks old.

▼ Take your time when you choose your guinea pigs. Make sure you pick the liveliest puppies of the litter.

to handle the guinea pigs so that you can be sure
are in good health. If you are choosing two
make sure they are either males (boars)
males (sows) from the same litter.
u want more than two, choose sows
ey may be less likely to fight.

out what food your pets are used
d ask for a little of their bedding
t in their new hutch.

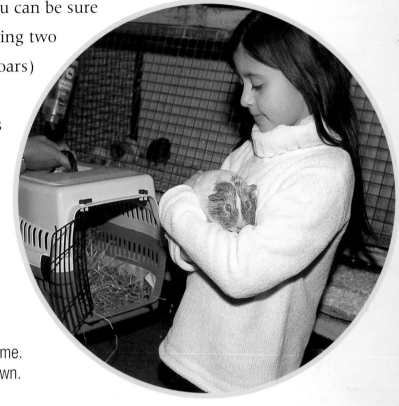

e an animal carrier to take your new pets home.
some hay inside so that they can nestle down.

op Tips

en choosing your guinea pigs,
k for the following:

Clean, shiny fur with no bare or
damp patches;

a rounded, plump, and firm body;

shiny eyes and clean nose, ears,
and mouth;

liveliness!

e how this guinea pig's
es shine! A healthy, alert
imal like this one will
ake a wonderful pet.

A home for your pets

Have a hutch ready for your new guinea pigs.

For two pigs, the hutch should be at least five feet (1.5 m) long, two feet (60 cm) wide, and two feet (60 cm) high. It needs a dark sleeping area and a daytime area with a wire-mesh door to let in light and air. The hutch should also be raised off the ground, on legs or bricks, to keep it dry. It is best to put the hutch indoors—a shed is ideal.

▲ When you get your new pe home, put them right into hutch. Stay low to the gro when handling guinea pig: high fall could kill them.

en the weather is not too cold,
can put the hutch outside.
e sure the hutch is properly
therproofed, and put it
ewhere that is shaded from
sun and sheltered from
wind.

▲ Your new pets will want to explore their surroundings. Leave them alone for a few hours while they get used to their new home.

Top Tips

Weather beaters

🐾 If the hutch is outside, cover it with plastic when there is heavy rain. Make sure you remove it and check for dampness afterward.

🐾 Never put the hutch in a garage used by cars. Exhaust fumes could kill your pets.

🐾 Do not put the hutch in a greenhouse. Your pets could overheat and die.

▼ Guinea pigs cannot stand too much cold—or too much heat. Put your pets' hutch outside only in mild weather, and make sure there is some shelter from the sun.

Inside the hutch

Make the hutch into a cozy home for your pets.

Line the floor with sheets of newspaper. You ca[n] add wood shavings if you want, but never put sawdust in your pets' hutch—it can damage th[e] eyes and lungs. Fill the sleeping area with shredded paper and hay. Your guinea pigs will like to eat and play with the hay, as well as sle[ep] in it. Do not use straw instead of hay. It is cheaper but is not good for your pets.

▼ Guinea pigs love to explore. A plastic tube makes a perfect toy.

ach a water bottle to the mesh door and the food bowls inside the hutch. Add a t-tree branch for your guinea pigs to aw—this will keep their teeth trimmed.

▲ Pet guinea pigs need lots of hay to nibble. Add fresh hay every day.

Checklist: hutch kit

Plastic drip-feed water bottle with a netal spout

Pottery food bowls—one for dried and ne for fresh food

Bedding, such as shredded white paper

• Hay

• Sheets of old newspaper

• Fruit-tree branch or gnawing block

• Tubes or boxes to explore—cardboard is fine, or you can buy tough plastic ones

• Wood shavings

Feeding your guinea pigs

Like you, your guinea pigs should not miss meals.

It is your job to feed your pets. Give th[e] special guinea pig food, which is a mix[ture] dried plants, seeds, and vegetables. You must make sure they always have drie[d] food to eat.

▲ Feeding time! Check on the package or with your vet to find out how much dried food to give your guinea pigs.

your pets at the same time
day. In addition to the food
add an extra handful of hay for
to nibble. For a special treat,
handfeeding some shelled,
alted peanuts.

ng dry food is thirsty work, so
your pets' water bottle full. You
uld also give them fresh fruit
vegetables (*see page 14*).

▲ Remember to refill your guinea pigs' water bottle with fresh water every day.

op Tips

eeding kit

- Put your pets' food in heavy, pottery bowls that cannot be tipped.

- Always throw away any leftover food from the day before.

- Do not put anything plastic in the hutch unless it has been made for guinea pigs. Your pets will gnaw it.

stay healthy, a guinea
ig needs a mix of dried
ood, fresh hay, and raw
egetables or fruit.

Get fresh!

Guinea pigs love eating fresh fruit and vegetables.

Like you, they need vitamin C, so you should give them some fresh food every day. About a handful for each pig is enough—more might give them upset tummies. Always wash any fresh food first.

Give a mix of foods. Chop up vegetables such as carrots, celery, cucumbers, or corn-on-the-cob. Your guinea pigs will also enjoy a small piece of apple, pear, or even orange. Try hiding the fresh food and see how long it takes your pets to sniff it out. Remember where you've put it, though. You should take out any uneaten fresh food after a day, before it spoils.

▶ This guinea pig is enjoying a piece of broccoli. You will soon find out which fruits and vegetables are your pets' favorites.

14

Want to know a great way to make friends with your new pet? Handfeed it a slice of delicious apple!

Checklist: wild plants

You could give your guinea pigs food from the wild. Try freshly picked

- Chickweed
- Clover
- Dandelions
- Grass
- Groundsel
- Lamb's quarters
- Plantain
- Shepherd's purse
- Yarrow

Don't pick weeds from beside the road—they will have poisons on them from all the car exhaust.

Handling

Handle each of your guinea pigs every day.

For the first couple of days, just talk to your pets so that they get used to your voice. Then you can begin to handle them. Always sit down to hold a guinea pig so it is safely cradled in your lap. Cup your hands to support its body. Remember to talk softly—your pet will like the sound of your voice.

◄ Make sure to support your gu[inea] pig's body as yo[u] hold it close to y[our] chest or lap.

not to make any jerky movements
might startle your guinea pig.
't handle your pets too soon after
have fed them. Give them time for
tummies to settle first.

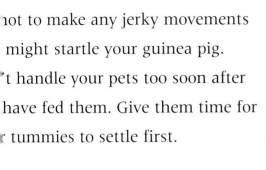

▶ Give your guinea pigs plenty of
attention each day, and spend the same
amount of time handling each one.

Pet Talk

uinea pig hairstyles

ere are three types of guinea pig hair: short,
g, and rough. If your guinea pig is long-
ired or rough-haired, you will need to brush
coat every day. Short-haired pigs like being
ushed, too. Get a soft baby brush and use it
ly for grooming your guinea pigs.

en you groom your pet, brush
ntly. Move the brush down the
ck away from the head.

Great outdoors

Your guinea pigs will enjoy getting out in the fresh air.

On nice days, you can let your pets ou[t] a triangular-shaped run called a "grazi[ng] ark." First check that the grass has no[t] been treated with weedkiller.

Choose an ark with a raised nesting ar[ea] at one end. Put in some hay for your guinea pigs to nestle in when they wa[nt] to take a nap. Move the ark around the lawn every few days to give your guine[a] pigs fresh grass to nibble. They will ne[ed] dried food, too, and their water bottle.

▼ Put fresh hay in the ark for your guinea pigs. Guinea pigs need to have hay all the time—even when there is plenty of grass to eat!

Pet Talk

...you also have a pet rabbit, you can put it in the grazing ark ...th the guinea pigs. You will need to supervise them, though, ...d supply them with separate food. Your rabbits and guinea ...gs should not share the same hutch. They need their own ...ace and might fight if they have to be together all the time.

▲ Your grazing ark should have a shaded area at one end where your pets can escape from the sun. You can let guinea pigs and rabbits share the ark, as long as you stay there to watch over them.

Remember to attach a full water bottle to the side of the ark.

Guinea pig talk

Your guinea pigs will try to talk to you!

When your pets hear you coming, they might "squeak" to get your attention. They also make "cooing" noises to reassure each other. Listen for "purring" and "chirping." Your guinea pigs make these noises when they are happy.

▶ Your guinea pig will love being stroked and may make purring noises if it is relaxed. It is a great way for you to make friends with your pet.

Pet Talk

Guinea pigs have a keen sense of smell. That is how they recognize each other—and you! They also mark their territory with scent. They have scent glands on their cheeks, backs, and bottoms.

▲ Guinea pigs can be real chatterboxes! Listen to the noises your pets make to each other.

When guinea pigs are annoyed, they make a chattering sound. This might be a sign that your pets are going to fight. It should not happen if you choose pigs from the same litter. Another noise you might hear is a frightened squeal. If this happens when you are handling your guinea pig, gently put it back in its hutch.

▼ These guinea pigs are saying "Hello!" to each other.

Cleaning up

Keep your guinea pig's hutch clean—or it will smell bad.

Check the hutch every day. You should remove any leftover food, droppings, or wet bedding. Wash the food bowl and water bottle, too.

Once a week, give the hutch a thorough cleaning. First, put your guinea pigs somewhere safe—a cardboard box or pet carrier is ideal. Empty out all the hay, shredded paper, and newspaper.

▲ It is a good idea to wear rubber gloves when you are cleaning out the hutch.

sh or scrape any dirt from the floor. Now you can put
n fresh newspaper and fill the nesting area with clean
and shredded paper.

ry couple of months,
b the hutch with
cial pet disinfectant.
se away any traces
disinfectant, then let
hutch dry out
pletely.

ake sure the hutch is fully dry before
tting down newspaper and bedding.

Checklist: cleaning kit

se these things only for cleaning out your
uinea pig hutch:

Rubber gloves

Dustpan and brush

Scraper

Scrubbing brush

Plastic bowl or bucket for hot water

Pet disinfectant

Soap

Sponge

Bottle brush

Rags or paper towels

Healthy pets

If you look after your pets, they will probably stay healthy.

If you have a cold, stay away from your pets—they could catch it, too. Take sick guinea pigs to the vet as soon as possible.

Even healthy guinea pigs need a yearly check-up with the vet. He or she will also cut their claws or teeth if they have grown too long.

▶ When you are handling your pet, check its fur for little insects called "mites."

not a good idea to try to breed
nea pigs. There are too many
vanted pets. But there is no need to
e your pets neutered. Just keep
m away from guinea pigs of the
osite sex.

Checklist:

you see any of these signs of illness, take
ur guinea pig to the vet:

Dull fur

Sores on its skin

Dirty ears or eyes

Sneezing

Lots of scratching

Noisy breathing or wheezing

Shivering

Diarrhea (upset tummy)

Little insects (mites) in the fur

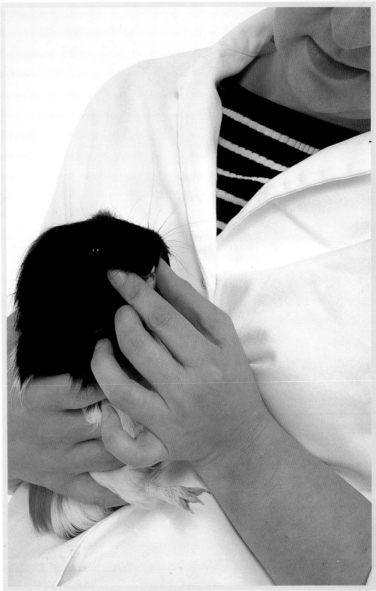

▲ Ask an adult to check your guinea
pig's teeth. They should not be
overgrown. If they are, you will
need to take your pet to the vet.

◀ Long claws need to be cut, but
this is a job for the vet. Never try
to cut your pets' claws.

Vacation time

When you go on vacation, do not forget your pets.

Ask a friend to come and feed your guinea pigs once a day. They will also need to add fresh water and clean the hutch. It might be easier to take pets and all their equipment to your friend's house.

▼ Make sure your friend knows how to look after your pet while you are away on vacation.

...e a list of what to do and add your vet's telephone
...ber, just in case. Show your friend how to handle the
...—gently and firmly, but without squeezing. If you
...ot find anyone to care for your guinea pigs, see if
...r vet or local pet shop can help you.

▶ Give your friend a list of your
guinea pigs' favorite foods.

Pet Talk
Meeting other animals

If your friend has guinea pigs, he or she will
know how to look after yours. Guinea pigs do
not get along with cats or dogs, though. If
your friend has these, make sure they are
kept away from your pets.

◀ Your pets could share a grazing ark
with your friend's—as long as there is
someone watching over them to make
sure they do not fight.

Guinea pig facts

Bet you didn't know that the Incas used to breed guinea pigs for eating! Read on for more fantastic facts.

• Guinea pigs are not related to pigs, even though the males are called "boars" and the females are called "sows."

• Guinea pigs are rodents, related to rats and mice. Like all rodents, they have teeth that never stop growing.

• Guinea pigs are from a family of animals called "cavies." They are related to capybaras and pacas of South America.

ild guinea pigs spend about six hours
ng each day. They usually feed at dawn
dusk, when the dim light makes it hard
hunting animals to spot them.

uinea pigs sleep for about five hours
y, but they never close their eyes
more than 10 minutes.

ild guinea pigs live in family groups of
ut 10 animals called "colonies."

here are around 50 different breeds of
hestic (pet) guinea pig.

other guinea pigs grunt to call their
ies; they have one to four young.

• Unlike many rodent babies, guinea pigs are
already furry when they are born—and their
eyes are open, too.

Glossary

Boar
A male guinea pig.

Breeder
Someone who keeps guinea pigs to mate them and produce babies to sell. He or she will want to produce puppies of a particular breed or type.

Colony
A group of guinea pigs that live together.

Disinfectant
A cleaning fluid that kills germs. Ask your vet or pet shop for a mild disinfectant that is suitable for cleaning your guinea pigs' hutch. Follow the instructions with care.

Grazing ark
A triangular run, made of wire mesh, that you can put your guinea pigs in so that they can graze on your lawn. The ark should have a shaded area at one end.

Grooming
Brushing a guinea pig's fur. Long-haired or rough-haired guinea pigs need to be brushed every day.

Litter
A group of animals all born at the same time to the same mother. They are brothers and sisters.

Neutering
Removing an animal's sex organs so that it cannot have babies.

Pedigree
A particular type of guinea pig, such as an Abyssinian.

Puppy
A baby guinea pig.

Scent glands
Places on a guinea pig's body that produce a smell. Guinea pigs rub their cheeks, backs, and bottoms against things to mark their territory.

Sow
A female guinea pig.

Territory
The area of land that belongs to a colony of guinea pigs.

Further Information

Books

Baglio, Ben M. and Shelagh McNicholas. *Guinea Pig in the Garage*.
Pittsburgh: Apple, 2001.

Birmelin, Immanuel. *My Guinea Pig and Me*. Hauppauge, New York: Barrons, 2001.

Blackaby, Susan. *A Guinea Pig for You: Caring for Your Guinea Pig*.
Minneapolis: Picture Window Books, 2003.

Evans, Mark. *Guinea Pigs: ASPCA Pet Care Guide*. London: Dorling
Kindersley, 2001.

Foran, Jill. *Caring for Your Guinea Pig*.
Calgary: Weigl, 2004.

Holub, Joan. *Why Do Rabbits Hop?
And Other Questions About Rabbits,
Guinea Pigs, Hamsters, and Gerbils*.
New York: Dial, 2003.

Loves, June. *Guinea Pigs and Rabbits*.
Broomall, Penn.: Chelsea House, 2003.

Useful addresses

American Cavy Breeders Association
http://www.acbaonline.com/

**The American Society for the Prevention
of Cruelty to Animals (ASPCA)**
www.aspca.org

Humane Society of Canada
www.humanesociety.com

**Humane Society of the
United States**
www.hsus.org

Index